AURAL SURVIVAL BOOK

Grade 5

Caroline Evans

EDITION PETERS

LONDON • FRANKFURT/M • LEIPZIG • NEW YORK

Peters Edition Limited
2-6 Baches Street
London
N1 6DN
England

Tel: +44 (0)20 7553 4000
Fax: +44 (0)20 7490 4921
e-mail: sales@editionpeters.com
Internet: www.editionpeters.com

First published 2006
Revised edition published 2012

ISBN 978-1-84367-044-5

A catalogue record for this book is available from the British
Library

Cover design: www.adamhaystudio.com

Illustrations: Joy FitzSimmons

Printed in the UK by Halstan & Co Ltd, Amersham, Bucks.

CONTENTS

The *Aural Test Survival Book* offers a chapter-by-chapter look at responses to questions typically asked by examiners. The speed and accuracy of your responses will help you gain a better mark.

Key to Symbols

T Time

R Rhythm

I Interval

K Key

About ... the Aural Test Survival Book

Don't be scared of aural tests! The *Aural Test Survival Book* will help you improve your listening skills and prepare you for the aural test in your music exam. You can use this book with a teacher, parent or friend, or you can practise the exercises on your own.

This book will encourage you to listen to music more actively and give you confidence to tackle the aural tests in your exam.

Try to spend a little time on aural skills as part of your regular practice. You already have your examination pieces, studies and scales. Now here's your own book of aural skills!

Caroline Evans

A note to teachers

The material in the *Aural Test Survival Book* corresponds to the Associated Board's aural requirements for music examinations and is suitable for all instrumentalists. Many of the tests are common to other examination boards and so students preparing for any music exam will find the book useful.

You can try out the activities in your lessons, or you can set them for your students to complete at home. The format of the book encourages students to think in terms of four important elements of music: Time, Rhythm, Interval and Key.

When the examiner says:

"Here is a melody for you to repeat. Would you prefer to sing it or play it? . . . I'll play it twice. Here is the key-chord . . . and your starting note . . ."

What should you do?

Decide with your teacher long before the exam whether you are going to sing or play this test.

Sing the notes of the key-chord in your head, noting whether it is major or minor.

Listen carefully to the melody, focusing on the first part of the phrase in the first playing, and on the second part of the phrase in the second playing.

Concentrate on the rhythm as well as the pitch.

Sing or play exactly what you have just heard played on the piano. You may play your response on the piano or on your own instrument.

What you need to know

The examiner will ask whether you wish to sing or play this test.

An unaccompanied melody in a major or minor key (with up to three sharps or flats) will be played twice on the piano. It will have a range of up to an octave. Sing or play it at a different octave if necessary.

The examiner will always start by playing the key-chord and starting note. A count-in of two bars (for example: 1-2-3-1-2-3) will be given.

Your starting note will be the tonic, third or fifth note of the scale.

Sing or play in time with the speed indicated by the examiner.

If you are playing your response on a transposing instrument (for example, clarinet or trumpet), you will be told your playing key so that it will sound at the same pitch as the piano.

Work out the key signature for the named key before you start playing.

If necessary, the examiner will play the melody again and allow you a second attempt, although this will affect your mark.

How should you do it?

Before the music starts:

- Hum or play quietly your starting note.

While listening:

- As soon as the examiner gives the count-in, tap your toe gently in time right through to the end of the test.

- Follow the shape of the melody in your head or draw the shape in the air with your hand.

- Listen carefully to the rhythm as well as the note pitches – the rhythm is just as important.

- Listen to the key-chord and tonic note and keep them in mind throughout the test.

When you start singing or playing:

- Keep tapping your toe gently in time while singing or playing the melody.

- Don't pause after the examiner has finished playing the second time – come straight in and keep to the same speed as the examiner, particularly when the phrase ends on a long note.

- Sing "lah" to each note. If you prefer, you may hum or whistle, although it is hard to whistle accurately.

- If you hear *staccato* notes, sing or play short notes.

- Don't cut short any notes that are long.

At all times:

- **Stand tall**
- **Sound confident**
- **Sing/play out**

Training session

Play some major and minor scales (with key signatures of up to three sharps or flats) on your own instrument (if voice is your instrument, then sing). Play at a comfortable speed and tap your toe gently to keep in time. Here are G major (ascending) and D harmonic minor (descending).

f you play a bass-clef instrument, here are he same scales in the bass clef:

/hen you have played each scale, sing it. n order for it to be comfortable for your ɔice, you may need to sing it an octave igher or lower than you played it.

ɛep to the speed you played before, and ill tap your toe gently to keep in time. ng "lah" or "doh" to each note, and make re each note is separated.

Test 5A

Repeat this exercise with some major and minor arpeggios. Here are A major ascending, and C minor descending:

Here are the same arpeggios in the bass clef:

As you sing and play, try to see the shape of the music in your head. For example, if you play an ascending and descending scale, it will look like this:

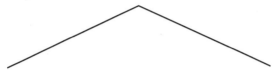

In a scale, the pattern of the notes is said to be "scalic" i.e. moving by step. In an arpeggio, the pattern is said to be "arpeggiated."

Look at the following music. The notes are the same as those in the major scale you played and sung on page 7:

G. F. Handel

Here is the same music in the bass clef:

Notice the scalic pattern of the notes. Start by clapping, or tapping on your side, the rhythm of the notes printed. Keep to the same speed as before.

Now play the music on your instrument, singing the phrase afterwards. Begin by dividing the melody into two 2-bar phrase so that you expand your musical memory gradually.

Now look away from the music and try to play and sing the phrase from memory. Start with two bars at a time, then all four. It may help if you try and visualise the fingering you would use.

Look at the following music. Notice the arpeggiated pattern of the notes. Most of the notes are the same as in the major arpeggio on page 8. First clap the rhythm, then play the music on your instrument, then sing the phrase. Count yourself in, before you start to play.

J. S. Bach

Here is the same music in the bass clef:

Now look away from the music and try to play and sing the whole phrase from memory.

How to improve further

Listen to some music you don't know and sing or play back short phrases. You could use the radio or TV and press the mute button while you sing or play.

The aim of the test

The purpose of this test is to develop your sense of pitch and rhythm, and expand your musical memory.

Quiz

Would you describe the opening of the following melodies as mostly "scalic" or "arpeggiated"? Answers on page 36.

- Yesterday.
- Jerusalem.
- Greensleeves.

1. Take a deep breath before you begin to sing so that you don't run out of air in the middle of the phrase.

2. Don't worry about the sound of your own voice – concentrate on singing in tune and in time.

3. Use bright vowels – "lah" is usually best and don't slide up or down the notes.

4. Concentrate on the first two bars in the first playing, the second two bars in the second playing.

5. Sing or play something, even if you're unsure – just get the rhythm right and end on the tonic.

6. Ask for a second attempt, if you feel that would achieve a better result, although this will affect your mark.

Follow the TRaK:

T Time: tap your toe in time while listening, singing or playing

R Rhythm: listen carefully to the rhythm as well as the note pitches and don't cut long notes short

K Key: listen carefully to the key-chord and starting note so that you sing in tune. If you play the test, work out the key signature for the named key first

SING AT SIGHT

When the examiner says:

"Would you prefer to sing notes in the treble clef or bass clef? . . . Please sing the notes at number . . . on this page. Sing them slowly, and I'll help by giving you the right note if you sing a wrong one. Here is the key-chord . . . and this is your starting note . . ."

What should you do?

Decide with your teacher before the exam whether you will sing this test from the treble or bass clef. Tell the examiner on the day.

Look carefully at the notes in the score. Then sing each note in succession on your own. Sing in free time.

What you need to know

The test will consist of six notes written as semibreves, within a range of a fifth above and a fourth below the tonic.

The test will not contain any intervals greater than a third, except a rising fourth (dominant to tonic).

The examiner will start by naming and playing the key-chord and starting note.

The key-signature will contain no more than two sharps or flats. The test will be in a major key, and your starting note and finishing note will be the tonic.

The music will have no time signature. This is known as free time and means that you can sing at your own pace.

If necessary, the examiner will help you by playing and naming the correct note if you sing a note incorrectly.

How should you do it?

While preparing:

- Listen to the key-chord. The first note (tonic) of the chord is your starting note. Sing the notes of the key-chord in your head as soon as they are played.

- Look to see if any notes in the score are in the key-chord which you have just heard.

- Look at the key signature. Check to see if it affects any notes in the test.

- Hum quietly to yourself as you work out interval steps or leaps. Do this by humming up or down from the preceding note, or from the tonic. Use sol-fa if you know it, or you could use the opening interval of a well-known melody (see page 14).

- Look carefully before you attempt to sing. Don't guess – you have time to think.

When you start singing:

- There is no need to sing in semibreves. Sing slowly in your own time – but don't take too long!

- Sing "lah" to each note. If you prefer, you may hum or whistle, although it is difficult to whistle accurately.

- Keep the starting note (tonic) in your head and be aware of the key throughout the piece.

- The first and last notes will be the tonic so there are only four more notes to work out!

- Remember also that the notes in this test will always move by step and small leaps. Try to hear the notes in your head before you sing.

Training session

Play the scales, one octave only, of C, G, D, F and B♭ major. If voice is your instrument, then sing. Play at a comfortable tempo. Here are D major ascending and B♭ major descending:

If you play a bass-clef instrument, here are the same scales in the bass clef:

Now play the arpeggios of C, G, D, F and B♭ major, at a comfortable tempo. Here are G major ascending and D major descending:

Here are the same arpeggios in the bass clef:

Now look at the intervals between notes. The aural test will only contain intervals within the scales and arpeggios you have just played. Here are the beginning of the major scale and the major arpeggio showing the intervals of a minor second (semitone), major second (tone), minor third, major third and perfect fourth:

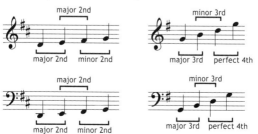

Test 5B

If you know sol-fa, you may find it helpful in this test. Otherwise, associating an interval with a well-known tune makes it easier to sing without having to count the interval. Here are the opening phrases of some well-known tunes with the intervals of the first two notes indicated.

All through the night:

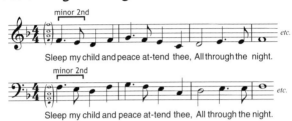

Sleep my child and peace at-tend thee, All through the night.

Sleep my child and peace at-tend thee, All through the night.

Frère Jacques:

Frè - re Jac-ques, frè - re Jac-ques, dorm-ez vous...

Frè - re Jac-ques, frè - re Jac-ques, dorm-ez vous...

Daisy, Daisy:

Dai - sy, Dai - sy, give me your ans-wer, do.

Dai - sy, Dai - sy, give me your ans-wer, do.

Swing low:

Swing low, sweet cha - ri - ot,___

Swing low, sweet cha - ri - ot,___

Here comes the bride (Wagner's *Bridal March*):

Play these phrases on your instrument and sing them back like an echo. Play the notes of the key-chord first. Once you have sung the whole phrase, sing just the first two notes that make the interval. Then sing the two notes in reverse order.

Here are six semibreves, similar to what you will see in the aural test. Play the notes of the key-chord, and then sing the notes slowly. The intervals are marked to help you. Think about the well-known tune for each interval.

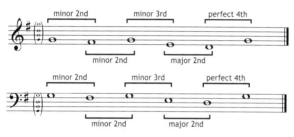

Here is another example. This time you need to work out the intervals for yourself. Play the key-chord before singing:

How to improve further

Look at any piece of music you are learning and try to sight-sing the first bar of any line. Ignore the rhythm and concentrate on pitching the notes accurately. Then try sight-singing the first bar of another line.

The aim of the test

This test develops your "inner ear", which helps you to hear the sound in your head before singing or playing.

1. Look carefully at each interval before you sing it. Don't guess.

2. Don't worry about the sound of your voice: concentrate on singing in tune.

3. Use bright vowels – "lah" is usually best (not "ler").

4. Take a deep breath before you start.

5. When singing a descending minor third, imagine calling for a lost dog or cat (e.g. "Ro-ver" or "Fe-lix") – or a two-tone siren.

6. It may help to follow the shape of the phrase with your hand as you sing.

Learn the TRIK:

T Time: you have time to think

R Rhythm: you don't have to worry about rhythm in this test

I Interval: work out the interval steps and leaps

K Key: listen carefully to the key-chord and starting note. Look carefully at the key signature. Sing the notes in your head as soon as the chord is played so that you sing in tune

When the examiner says:

"Listen to this piece, then I'll ask you about . . . and about style and period."

What should you do?

The examiner will play a short piece of music and then ask you one or two short questions about two features. The first feature will be one of the following:

Loud or quiet
(sometimes described as dynamics)

Gradually getting louder or quieter
(sometimes described as gradation of tone)

Detached, smooth or accented
(sometimes described as articulation)

Faster or slower
(sometimes described as tempo changes)

Major or minor
(sometimes described as tonality)

Character
(sometimes described as mood)

The second feature will be:

Style and period
(when the music was composed)

What you need to know

Try to know the meaning of the following Italian words. But if you can't remember the Italian word, use the English.

Loud or quiet
fairly loud; loud; very loud
Italian: *mezzo forte*; *forte*; *fortissimo*
symbols: *mf*; *f*; *ff*

fairly quiet, quiet, very quiet
Italian: *mezzo piano*; *piano*; *pianissimo*
symbols: *mp*; *p*; *pp*

Gradually getting louder or quieter

gradually getting louder
Italian: *crescendo*
symbol: ▭◁ (an "opening hairpin")

gradually getting quieter
Italian: *diminuendo*
symbol: ▷▭ (a "closing hairpin")

Detached or smooth

detached
Italian: *staccato*
symbol: ♩ ♪

smooth
Italian: *legato*
symbol: ⌒ (a slur)

accented notes
Italian: *sforzando*; *tenuto*
symbols: *sfz*, *sf*; ♩ ♪

Faster or slower

gradually getting faster
Italian: *accelerando* (*accel.*) or *stringendo*

gradually getting slower
Italian: *rallentando* (*rall.*) or *ritardando*
(*ritard.*)

Tonality

major or minor

Character

Describe the character or mood of the
piece, using words like:

sad (*mesto*)	playful (*scherzando*)
majestic (*maestoso*)	mysterious (*misterioso*)
calm (*tranquillo*)	energetic (*energico*)

rhythmic contrasts

song-like (*cantabile*) melody

Style and period

Style is the manner of writing, or what

the music sounds like. Use words like: dissonance, "bluesy" melody, off-beat accents, clearly-defined phrases.

Here are the main musical periods, with approximate dates:

Baroque: 1600-1750
Classical: 1750-1790
Romantic: 1790-1910
Early 20th century: 1910-1940
Contemporary: 1940-now

How should you do it?

Before the music starts:

* You only need to listen for two features. One will be style and period. The examiner will tell you which other feature to listen for BEFORE the music starts. Be prepared to answer additional questions about each feature.

While listening:

* Concentrate only on the particular features specified.

* If you are asked about a change from major to minor, you can indicate where it happens by raising your hand.

* Work out what time the music is in at this stage: you will be asked about it later (see page 29).

When you answer:

* Try to use Italian words like *sforzando*, *diminuendo*, *legato* and *pianissimo* in your answers.

* If you are describing the character of the piece, think about its mood.

* If you are describing the style of the piece, think also of the period in which it might have been composed.

- Use simple statements and respond straight away.
- Try to give two descriptions in your answers to character, and style and period.

Training session

You will not be expected to identify the composer of the piece nor be an expert in the history of music – just to indicate in which period you think the music was composed. It's a good idea to relate what you hear to what you know: ask yourself if it sounds similar to music you have sung, played or heard.

Here are some typical features of musical styles to listen out for. They will help you work out when a piece was composed.

BAROQUE (c.1600–c.1750)

Dynamics: restrained

Articulation: ornaments (turns, mordents, etc.); often lightly detached

Tonality: major or minor

Character: elegant phrases; often energetic, dotted rhythms

Style: dance forms like gavotte, minuet; limited range of the piano, no pedalling

Composers: J. S. Bach, Handel, Vivaldi, Purcell, D. Scarlatti, Couperin, Corelli

CLASSICAL (c.1750–c.1790)

Dynamics: more contrasted than in baroque music

Articulation: accented notes (e.g. *sforzando*); some ornaments (e.g. trills)

Tonality: major and minor

Character: balanced phrases, often flowing melodies

Style: tonal, graceful melodies, clearly-defined phrases, some pedalling

Composers: Haydn, Mozart, Beethoven, Dussek, Clementi

ROMANTIC (c.1790–c.1910)

Dynamics: contrasted; extensive use of *cresc.* and *dim.*

Articulation: flamboyant flourishes

Tempo: *rubato* is common

Tonality: chromaticism; modulations to unexpected keys

Character: lyrical; rich harmonic writing; irregular rhythmic groupings

Style: dance forms (like waltzes and mazurkas); descriptive music (describing emotions or things like waterfalls and reflections); uses wide range of the piano; considerable use of the pedal

Composers: Schubert, Chopin, Schumann, Tchaikovsky, Brahms, Grieg, Mendelssohn

EARLY 20TH CENTURY (c.1910–c.1940)

Dynamics: wide dynamic range; extremities of instrument used

Articulation: clearly defined and specific

Tonality: dissonance and chord clusters; use of pentatonic scales; atonal (no fixed key); large intervals and disjointed melody; modal

Character: large, powerful chords; changes of metre; complex rhythm; syncopation

Style: impressionism; jazz; folk

Composers: Debussy, Ravel, Gershwin, Stravinsky, Prokofiev, Shostakovich, Bartók

CONTEMPORARY (c.1940–now)

Dynamics: varied and contrasted

Articulation: varied

Tonality: major and minor; modal

Character: repetition of short rhythms; cross-rhythms; "bluesy" chords

Style: lyrical, influenced by other styles (world music, jazz, rock)

Composers: Steve Reich, John Tavener, Philip Glass, Michael Nyman, Richard Rodney Bennett

The following piece of music uses the notes of the key-chord of C major. Play the melody line on your instrument, or sing it. Keyboard players can play both parts.

Here is the melody in the bass clef:

Now play it with a variety of dynamics:

Answer these questions about what you have just played:

"What was the starting dynamic of this phrase? Did it change anywhere?"

Now play it with some articulation:

Answer these questions:

"Was the upper part played smoothly or with detached notes? Were the accents regular or syncopated?"

Now vary the speed of your playing:

Answer this question about what you have just played:

"Did the tempo vary or did it stay the same?"

When you change from a major to a minor key, one note in the key-chord changes. Which one is it? Is it raised or lowered by a semitone?

The piece you have just been playing is in a major key (sometimes called a major mode). Now play this version, which is in a minor key (or minor mode). Watch out for the key signature:

Now answer these questions about this piece:

"What in the music gives this piece its character?"

"Is this a Romantic, early 20th century, or more recent piece of music? Which musical features indicate that?"

Listen to some music on the TV, radio or on a CD or mp3 player. Decide whether the music you are listening to is:

fairly loud (*mezzo forte*), loud (*forte*) or very loud (*fortissimo*), or fairly quiet (*mezzo piano*), quiet (*piano*) or very quiet (*pianissimo*)

getting gradually louder (*crescendo*) or gradually quieter (*diminuendo*)

detached (*staccato*), smooth (*legato*), accented or ornamented

getting gradually faster (*accelerando*) or gradually slower (*rallentando*)

in a major or minor key

And, lastly, how would you describe the character or mood? Always try to give two descriptions in your answer. Here are some possibilities:

calm (*tranquillo*)	agitated (*agitato*)
reflective	playful (*scherzando*)
sad (*mesto*)	light (*leggiero*)
graceful (*grazioso*)	lively (*vivace*)
sweet (*dolce*)	forceful (*con forza*)
jazzy or "bluesy"	march-like (*marziale*)
tonal	discordant
syncopated	legato

Practise saying the answers out loud even if you are on your own. This is important because saying the answer is very different from thinking about the answer.

Here are some examples of questions you might be asked, and the sort of words you could use to answer them:

Loud or quiet (dynamics)

Question: "How would you describe the dynamics in the opening phrases of this piece?"

Answer: "They were all either very loud (*fortissimo*) or very quiet (*pianissimo*)."

Question: ". . . and did the phrase at the end become suddenly or gradually loud?"

Answer: "It became gradually loud – there was a *crescendo*."

Detached or smooth (articulation)

Question: "The upper part was *legato*. How were the lower notes played?"

Answer: "They were all accented, or *marcato*."

Question: "In the final phrase, was the articulation smooth or detached?"

Answer: "Detached"

Faster or slower (tempo)

Question: "Were there any changes in tempo or did it stay the same throughout?"

Answer: "The phrases got faster then slower – they were played with *rubato*."

Question: ". . . and then what happened to the tempo in the final bars?"

Answer: "It got gradually slower towards the end – there was a *ritardando*."

Major or minor tonality

Question: "Did the music end in a major key or in a minor key?"

Answer: "In a minor key."

Question: "Was this piece in a major key or a minor key?"

Answer: "Major."

Character or mood

Question: "What in the music gives this piece its character?"

Answer: "I thought the legato melody sounded quite reflective and calm."

Question: "What in the music gives this piece its character?"

Answer: "It had a lively and syncopated rhythm in a major key."

Question: "What in the music gives this piece its character?"

Answer: "It had loud, thick chords and was bold and fast."

Style and period

Question: "Is the style and period of this music Classical, Romantic or 20th century?"

Answer: "I think it was probably composed in the first half of the 20th century."

Question: "Which features in the music make you think that?"

Answer: "The clashing, dissonant chords and the contrasted dynamics."

How to improve further

Every time you hear any music (for example, on the TV or radio), try to listen carefully to one or two musical features – loud/quiet, detached/smooth, major/minor or faster/slower. Think also about the character and mood, style and period. Then describe the features out loud.

See if you can describe the pieces you are learning at the moment as fully as possible

Try listening to the following music and see if you can identify some of the typical features from each period:

BAROQUE: Vivaldi, *Four Seasons*; J.S. Bach, *Prelude in C, BWV 939*
CLASSICAL: Mozart, *Symphony No.40*; Clementi, *Sonatina, Op. 36, No.1*
ROMANTIC: Mendelssohn, ballet, *'A Midsummer Night's Dream'*; Chopin, *Prelude in D♭ major, Op. 28, No.15 'Raindrop'*
EARLY 20TH CENTURY: Holst, *'The Planets' Suite*, Op. 32; Debussy, *Children's Corner*
CONTEMPORARY: Philip Glass, *String Quartet No.1*; Richard Rodney Bennnett, *Diversion No.5*

The aim of the test

The purpose of this test is to develop your aural perception. It encourages you to listen to music rather than just hearing it.

1. Remember to work out what time the piece is in at the start of this test and keep it in your head for test 5C(ii) (see page 29). Remember that the first beat of the bar will be slightly accented.

2. When describing the character of a piece, don't be afraid of saying what immediately comes into your head. If it sounds spooky or dreamy, jumpy or cool, say so. If it sounds plain and simple, or jazzy, say so but say SOMETHING – you may get something right. If you say nothing you will get nothing right.

3. The second question in this test will always be about style and period.

4. If you can't decide when a piece was composed, start by deciding when it wasn't composed.

5. It doesn't matter if you can't remember the Italian term – say it in English.

> marcato
> tenuto
> baroqu
> classica

6. The questions you will be asked usually require only one-word answers or simple statements.

Put the music into words in the following categories:

- Dynamics, articulation and tempo
- Tonality and character
- Style and period

When the examiner says:

"Now clap the rhythm of the notes in this phrase, after I've played it twice more . . . Is it in two time, three time or four time?"

What should you do?

Clap the rhythm of a short extract from the same piece in 2-, 3- or 4-time.

Try to tap the beat with your toe while the music is played and keep tapping your toe when you are clapping the rhythm.

Begin clapping immediately the examiner has finished playing, keeping to the same speed as the examiner.

You will then be asked to state the time. In other words, say whether there are 2, 3 or 4 beats in a bar.

What you need to know

The examiner will play either the upper or lower part: in other words, an unaccompanied line of music from the same piece as you heard in test 5C(i). It will be played twice.

You are not required to give the full time signature; only to say if the piece is in 2-, 3- or 4-time.

The phrase may begin on an upbeat (anacrusis).

How should you do it?

Before the music starts:

- Put your hands in position, ready to start clapping.

While listening:

- Recall the time of the piece, which was played in full in the first part of the test.

- Count in your head to double-check the time.

- Gently tap your toe in time with the beat, right through to the end of the test.

- With your hands in the clapping position, silently tap your fingers on your palm when you hear the phrase played the second time.

When you start clapping:

- Clap the rhythm. Don't clap the beat.

- Clap firmly and precisely.

- Keep tapping the beat with your toe if you can – your clapping will sound more rhythmical.

- Start clapping the rhythm immediately the examiner has finished playing it the second time, keeping to the same speed.

- When you have finished clapping, state whether there are 2, 3 or 4 beats in a bar.

At all times:

- **Stand tall**
- **Sound confident**
- **Speak out**

Training session

Music in 2-time

Sing or play the folk song *Lightly row*, and feel the strong beat falling on the first beat of the bar. If you can't remember the tune, here is the opening:

Light-ly row, light-ly row, float-ing down the ri-ver's way,

Here it is in the bass clef:

Light-ly row, light-ly row, float-ing down the ri-ver's way,

This piece is in cut common time, or 2/2, which is simple duple time.

Look at the rhythm again, choose a comfortable tempo and tap the beat with your toe. Then, while still tapping the beat, clap the rhythm.

Tapping the beat with your toe while clapping the rhythm is difficult at first, but gets easier with practice. Eventually, it will be automatic and will help you keep time in your pieces.

Music in 3-time

You may know the aria *La donna è mobile* from the opera *Rigoletto*. Sing or play it, and feel the strong beat falling on the first beat of the bar. Here is the opening:

La don-na è mo-bi-le, Qual pi-uma al ven - to,

Here is the opening in the bass clef:

La don-na è mo-bi-le, Qual pi-uma al ven - to,

La donna è mobile is in 3/4 – simple triple time, although it is sometimes written in 3/8. Look at the rhythm again, choose a comfortable tempo and tap the beat with your toe. Then, while still tapping the beat, clap the rhythm.

Music in 4-time

Now sing or play the carol *O come, all ye faithful*. Feel the strong beat falling on the first beat of the bar. Here is the opening:

O come, all ye faith-ful, joy-ful and tri-umph-ant,

Here is the opening in the bass clef:

O come, all ye faith-ful, joy-ful and tri-umph-ant,

O come, all ye faithful is in 4/4 – simple quadruple time. Look at the rhythm again, choose a comfortable tempo and tap the beat with your toe. Then, while still tapping the beat, clap the rhythm, watching out for the anacrusis, or upbeat at the start.

It is sometimes difficult to tell the difference between 2/4 (or 2/2) and 4/4 (or 4/2) time signatures – they can both feel like march-time. But if there is a clear emphasis on alternate beats, it is likely the piece will be in 2-time rather than 4-time.

How to improve further

Every time you hear any music on the TV, radio, CD or mp3 player, clap the rhythm of a small phrase. Press the mute button before you clap.

Practise tapping the beat with your toe at the same time as clapping the rhythm. Try and work out how many beats there are in a bar.

The aim of the test

This test is designed to develop a strong sense of rhythm and will help you play or sing your own pieces rhythmically and in time.

Quiz

Can you clap the rhythm of the following pieces? How many beats are there in a bar?

1. *Largo* from Dvořák's *New World Symphony*.

2. *Waltzing Matilda* – is it a waltz?

3. *Chim Chim Cher-ee* from Mary Poppins.

Answers on page 36.

SURVIVAL TIPS

1. Be sure to clap the rhythm, NOT the beat.

2. Be precise: when you clap, keep one hand still, palm upwards, and clap your other hand against it. If you have to clap a long note, keep your palms pressed together for the whole length of the note.

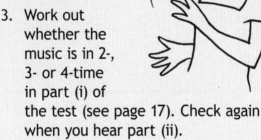

3. Work out whether the music is in 2-, 3- or 4-time in part (i) of the test (see page 17). Check again when you hear part (ii).

4. Be aware that the phrase might start on an upbeat.

Follow the TRaK:

T Time: tap your toe in time with the beat. Count the number of beats in a bar and state the time.

R Rhythm: be aware of how the rhythm fits with the beat, but be sure to clap the rhythm, not the beat.

K Key: you don't need to think about the key in this test.

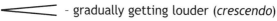

FIND OUT THE MEANING

◢◣ – gradually getting louder (*crescendo*)
◥◤ – gradually getting quieter (*diminuendo*)
> – accent

⌒ – slur. Notes within a slur should be smooth

Accelerando, stringendo – gradually getting faster
Agitato – agitated
Al fine – to the end
Anacrusis – upbeat at the beginning of a piece or phrase
Arpeggiated – like an arpeggio, moving by leap
Articulation – how the notes are played or sung (smoothly or detached)
Beat – a unit of time. In 4/4 time there are four crotchet beats in a bar. Sometimes the word "pulse" is used for "beat"
Binary form – AB structure; one section followed by a different second section
Con forza – forceful
Crescendo, cresc. – gradually getting louder
Diminuendo, dim. – gradually getting quieter
Dissonance – discordant, clashing
Dolce – sweet
Dominant – fifth note of the scale
Dynamics – how loudly or quietly the notes are played or sung
Energico – energetic
Forte, f – loud
Fortissimo, ff – very loud
Gavotte – baroque dance in two-time
Gradation of tone – the gradual increase or decrease of volume
Grazioso – graceful
Key – major or minor. It also applies to the sharps (♯) or flats (♭) in the key signature. "Sing in key" means sing in tune
Key-chord – first, third and fifth notes of the scale
Key note, tonic – first note of the scale, or home note
Legato – smooth
Leggiero – light

Maestoso - majestic, stately

Marcato - accented

Marziale - march-like, in a military style

Mesto - sad

Mezzo forte, mf - fairly loud

Mezzo piano, mp - fairly quiet

Minuet - baroque dance in three-time

Misterioso - mysterious

Modal - music based on a mode (e.g. dorian, aeolian) rather than a major or minor scale

Modulation - change of key

Mordent - an ornament where the printed note is rapidly followed by the note above (or below) then the printed note again

Pianissimo, pp - very quiet

Piano, p - quiet, soft

Pitch - how high or low a note is

Pulse - see *Beat*

Rallentando, ritardando - gradually getting slower

Rhythm - notes of varying lengths grouped into patterns

Rubato - slowing and quickening of tempo

Scalic - like a scale, moving by step

Scherzando - playful

Semitone - half a tone, minor second

Sforzando, sfz, sf - accented, forced

Staccato - detached

Stringendo - getting faster

Syncopation - when the rhythm emphasises off-beats

Tenuto - held

Tonality - major or minor

Tone - major second

Tonic - see *Key note*

Tranquillo - calm, tranquil

Trill - two rapidly alternating notes

Vivace - lively

Waltz - dance in 3-time

Note: The words used to introduce the tests may be slightly different to those used in this book.

Answers to quiz questions:

Page 9: scalic; arpeggiated; scalic

Page 33: 4-time; 4-time (not a waltz); 3-time